THE TANK RANGE PROJECT

By

Jamie Robinson & Roger Shank

GREY BRUCE ARTS COLLECTIVE

greybruceartscollective@gmail.com

www.greybruceartscollective.com

THIS IS A GREY BRUCE ARTS COLLECTIVE PRODUCTION

COPYRIGHT © 2013 BY JAMIE ROBINSON & ROGER SHANK

ALL RIGHTS RESERVED. PUBLISHED IN CANADA BY
DEUM PUBLICATIONS
A DIVISION OF THE DEUM FOUNDATION NOT_FOR PROFIT.

ALL RIGHTS RESERVED. WRITTEN PERMISSION MUST BE SECURED FROM THE PUBLISHER TO USE OR REPRODUCE ANY PART OF THIS BOOK, EXCEPT BRIEF, REFERENCED QUOTATIONS.

THIS PLAY IS SUBJECT TO ROYALTY. RIGHTS TO PRODUCE, FILM, OR RECORD, IN WHOLE OR IN PART, IN ANY MEDIUM OR ANY LANGUAGE, BY ANY GROUP, AMATEUR OR PROFESSIONAL, ARE RETAINED BY THE AUTHORS. THOSE INTERESTED IN OBTAINING AMATEUR OR PROFESSIONAL RIGHTS SHOULD CONTACT: GREYBRUCEARTSCOLLECTIVE@GMAIL.COM

ISBN: 0-9867451-1-1
EAN-13: 978-0-9867451-1-9

LIBRARY OF CONGRESS CATALOGING –IN-PUBLICATION
DATA AVAILABLE.

BOOK DESIGN BY MALIK HAKIM

PRINTED IN CANADA.

DEUM PUBLISHING
147 LIBERTY ST.
TORONTO, ONTATIO
M6K 3G3

TESTIMONIALS

"...A UNIQUE AND REFRESHING EXPERIENCE...
FABULOUS...
FOR THE MUNICIPALITY IT IS A WONDERFUL THING...
TO BRING OUR STORIES TO LIFE."

-Meaford Independent

"I FOUND THIS PLAY VERY POWERFUL."

-Doug Reid, local

"LOVED IT! I AM GLAD I WASN'T ONE OF THOSE PEOPLE LIVING ON THAT BEAUTIFUL LAND."

- Jeanne Johnson, local

DEDICATION

To all the farmers who sacrificed their land and the men and women they continue to support.

SPECIAL THANKS

Susan Turnbul for her dramaturgy throughout. Marjorie Davison, Rod MacAlpine, Karin Noble, Mel Smith, Pam Woolner, Corrine McGowen, Captain Ted Dinning and Captain Chris Carthew for their community advisory. Leata Ashby, Carrie Cowling and Don Cowling for their personal interviews. Lisa O'Connell, Brendan Rowland and Pat The Dog Playwright Centre for the Magnetic North Festival reading. Mark Rotil, John Dolan, Abigail Fernandes, Gord S. Miller, Leanna Brodie, Krista Hansen-Robitschek, Sarah Phillips and the Festival Players for their workshop read. Malik Hakim for this publication. Richard Greenblatt, Jonathan Duder, Diana Reimer, Iris Turcott and Keira Loughran for additional contributions. The Grey Roots Museum, rotary club of Meaford, Meaford Hall and Culture Foundation, Meaford Hall Arts and Cultural Centre, The Stratford Festival of Canada, The Stratford Festival Guthrie committee, SpringWorks indie theatre & arts festival, Canada Council for the arts and Ontario arts council.

Most thanks go to our always supportive partners, Lila Hakim and Julie Miles, and our children, Dorian Hakim Robinson, Eldon Shank and Annie-Irene Shank.

PRODUCTION HISTORY

The original staged reading of The Tank Range Project was performed for the 100 Mile Playwright Festival at The Meaford Hall Arts and Culture Centre on October 2nd, 2010 with the following cast and crew:

```
BLUE EYES...........................Tina Szyjak
VINCENT WHITELAW..............Dan Roberts
SARAH VAIL.........................Mackenzie Muldoon
ROBERT SPENCER/BOY 1........Gareth Potter
CARL/BOY 2.........................Ron Kennell
AUCTIONEER/SOLDIERS........Wayne Bryant
STAGE DIRECTIONS.............. Mary Bryant

DIRECTOR...........................Roger Shank
STAGE MANAGER.................Kristopher Weber
```

The World Premier of The Tank Range Project was performed at Stratford, Ontario's SpringWorks indie theatre & arts festival in May, 2012 with the following cast and crew:

```
BLUE EYES...........................Mackenzie Muldoon
VINCENT WHITELAW............Ryan Boyko
SARAH VAIL.........................Keira Loughran
ROBERT SPENCER................Eli Ham
CARL..................................Marvin Hinz
AUCTIONEER.......................Wilex Ly
BOY....................................Adam Lumsden
GIRL..................................Miranda Reynolds
SINGER..............................Adam Lumsden
AS CAST.............................Brett Brownlee, Vicky Laufer,
                                   Mandy London, Jannica Meyer

DIRECTORS..........................Jamie Robinson & Roger Shank
CHOREOGRAPHER................ Mandy London
MUSIC DIRECTOR..................Courtney Meloche
STAGE MANAGER..................Leslie Jost
```

The Tank Range Project

This published edition of The Tank Range Project was performed at Stratford, Ontario's SpringWorks indie theatre & arts festival and at The Meaford Hall Arts and Culture Centre in May, 2013 with the following cast and crew:

```
BLUE EYES……………………..Sophia Kolinas
VINCENT WHITELAW…………..Ryan Boyko
SARAH VAIL……………………..Mackenzie Muldoon
ROBERT SPENCER……………..Roger Shank
CARL…………………………….Marvin Hinz
AUCTIONEER…………………..Wilex Ly
BOY/SALES PITCH……………..Brett Brownlee
GIRL……………………………...Holly McCourt
AS CAST………………………...Mandy McDonald

DIRECTORS……………………..Jamie Robinson, Roger Shank & Eli Ham
SET DESIGN……………………..Adam Connor
STAGE MANAGER……………..Leslie Jost
```

COVER ART

Designed by Brett Brownlee.

PLAYWRIGHTS' NOTE

In the spirit of collective writing, we encourage all future productions to take the liberty of moulding these words to suit their individual needs. The only thing we ask is to preserve the truth of the story to the best of your ability, respecting the lives that were touched by this event. For further reading, we recommend the following books and links:

The Search for the Girl with the Blue Eyes: A Venture into Reincarnation, by Jess Stern.
St. Vincent: The Tree with the Broken Branch, by Marjorie Davison.
St. Vincent- A Beautiful Land, Conestoga Press.
www.greyroots.com/exhibitions/virtual-exhibits/home-on-the-range-the-meaford-tank-range-story/
www.greybruceartscollective.com/
www.meaford.com/atc2.html

DRAMATIS PERSONAE

(in order of appearance)

BLUE EYES

VINCENT WHITELAW

SARAH VAIL

ROBERT SPENCER

CARL

Soldiers, Girl, Boy, Auctioneer

FORWARD TO THE TANK RANGE PROJECT

1942 brought heart break and despair to 154 St. Vincent Township families living close to Georgian Bay in today's Municipality of Meaford. World War Two was raging and the Canadian Government made the decision to expropriate 17, 000 acres of valuable farmland to be used as a military training centre. Falsely promising the stricken landowners that the land would be returned to them at the end of the war, with great reluctance, the people sadly packed their belongings and tearfully left the land pioneered by their ancestors.

For 42 years, the gates of the Tank Range, as it was locally known, were closed to the general public. In 1984 during Ontario's Bicentennial year, permission was granted for a mammoth reunion of former and present St. Vincent residents to be held at the military base. It was an event long to be remembered. Close to 10,000 people joined in the festivities of the weekend event.

The years have passed. The children of 1942 are now the seniors of 2013. Memories are fading, the heart ache that existed for many years has gone. Newcomers are surprised to know that the land was once a thriving farming community with churches, schools, mills, and a dock at Cape Rich where lake boats docked regularly. Apple trees produced fruit famous for its quality, and the fishing industry was an economic asset. Its natural scenic beauty brought many tourists to the area, as well. All this we lost.

Today the Tank Range, as it was locally called, is known as the Land Forces Central Area Training Centre (LFCATC). Thousands of young cadets and army personnel have travelled over the land of St. Vincent's earliest settlers without realizing the angst of 1942, and have left to proudly represent Canada in Afghanistan and other war-torn countries.

To Roger Shank and the members of the Grey-Bruce Arts Collective, I offer congratulations and thank them for writing this play based on the historic saga of the Expropriation of 1942.

Marjorie Davison

Author: *St. Vincent- The Tree With the Broken Branch.*
Co- writer: *St. Vincent- A Beautiful Land.*

Jamie Robinson & Roger Shank

PROLOGUE.

Two Canadian soldiers enter in daylight unfolding a Concertainer unit (a temporary fortification structure) during the following advertisement:

SALES PITCH
(bold and engaging)
Considered to be the most significant development in field fortifications since World War II. Used by major military organizations around the world. Designed to replace conventional materials such as sandbags and soil. Build it. Fill it. It *will* protect you. Build a trench. Build a fort. The Theatre of War, as you've never seen it before!

The soldiers complete their construction of a fortified wall. One exits. The remaining female soldier, Blue Eyes, puts on her headphones. Peace.

She breaths in the air: sand, dust, coughing.

BLUE EYES
Sure not in Meaford, Ontario anymore. What am I doin' here? Don't train you for this heat. How do these people do it? Give me a lake, a pond, a creek, a puddle, something. Nope. Just white poppy fields for days. How can it be snowin' up there and like, fifty degrees down here? Damn, they don't train you for this.
Just do the job. People need their land protected, keep it out of enemy hands.
I am the land protector. I'm the King of the castle and you're the dirty rascal!
Could really use a...

Beat. Meditating.

BLUE EYES
Land Forces Central Area Training Centre
Land Forces Central Area Training Centre
Land Forces Central Area Training Centre

The Tank Range Project

    Meaford Meaford Meaford
    Canada Canada Canada
    Hockey Hockey Hockey.
    Cold mornin' drills around the lake.
    Cold Cool Mountain Lake.
    Ahh, that's good.

       Beat.

BLUE EYES
    Nooo, that's hot! It's too hot, and they keep fighting each other here for what? Land? We should just tell these people to look at a map of Southern Ontario, close their eyes and point, and there you go, land, land, land, we got land!
    Come on now, you're just homesick, you're too hot.

       In the distance, a tank turret gun aims out. Blue Eyes saunters next to it.

BLUE EYES
    At least I got you with me. L55 120mm smoothbore gun; slick, smooth, ride.

       Long beat as Blue Eyes closes her eyes and night begins to fall.

BLUE EYES
    I miss snow. Can't believe I'm saying it, but I miss the snow. Seein' them peaks up there coated with the white stuff. Skiin', trainin', buildin', fightin'.
    My protector.
    Look at that starlight.

       Blue Eyes sings along to a Sinatra tune.

       Suddenly, a distant headlight approaches.

BLUE EYES
    Stop that vehicle. Stop it now.

A diesel engine is heard quickly approaching her post. We hear an Arabic voice from offstage:

ARABIC VOICE
Man ooni ke haghan male mane az dast nemidam (*I will not surrender what is rightfully mine*)-

BLUE EYES
Do you understand me! Stop that vehicle now!-

ARABIC VOICE
-In zamine mane, mazraeye mane (*This is my land, my farm*)-

BLUE EYES
-We're here to help you, man!-

ARABIC VOICE
-Va barayash mi miram (*and I will die for it*)-

BLUE EYES
-You are trespassing on coalition soil! You must stop that thing now and leave the premises immediately, do you understand! We are *on your side*! I'm giving you five seconds-

ARABIC VOICE
-Man hagh daram ke inja bemanam (*I have a right to stay here*)-

BLUE EYES
-One-

ARABIC VOICE
-Jayi ke davazdah nasl ghabl az man boodeand (*where twelve generations have stayed before me*)-

BLUE EYES
-Two, three-

The Tank Range Project

ARABIC VOICE
-To bayasti khodeto taslim bokoni baraye pa gozashtan rooye zamine man! (*You should surrender for trespassing on my property!*)-

BLUE EYES
-Four-

> *Explosion. A muffled hum from the headphones plays. Blue Eyes hangs over the turret.*
>
> *A modern jet is heard flying slowly overhead. It magically transforms into an antiquated propeller driven plane.*

SCENE 1. "BALL OF FIRE"

> *1942. A barn dance.*
>
> *Vincent Whitelaw, stands alone by a haystack reading a book, flipping a dollar coin.*
>
> *Blue Eyes slowly comes to, mysteriously transported to 1942. She observes, unseen.*
>
> *Sarah Vail enters, knocking into Vincent, his coin disappearing. Blue Eyes discovers the coin in her hand and watches the scene unfold.*

VINCENT
Hey, watch where you're going there pal...

SARAH
This is a dance floor not a library.

VINCENT
Oh, uh, sorry, I...

> *Putting down his book, Vincent searches for the dollar.*

SARAH
Forget it, no big deal-

VINCENT
That's a whole dollar you made me lose.

SARAH
Well aren't you a ball of fire.

VINCENT
Ball of what?

SARAH
Ball of fire, you never hear of that before?

VINCENT
No I, I haven't.

Sarah flips through the book.

VINCENT
That dollar is...

SARAH
Say, what's this about?

VINCENT
What's what about?

SARAH
"The Second Part of Henry-"

VINCENT
Hey, give me that!

SARAH
Gee, how many parts does this Henry character have.

VINCENT
Henry the sixth.

SARAH
  Six parts!?

VINCENT
  No, the second part of King Henry...what, you never hear of Shakespeare before.

SARAH
  Confusing, you ask me.

VINCENT
  You always go around snooping through other people's stuff like that?

SARAH
  Only when I'm interested.

  Beat.

VINCENT
  You, uh, don't remember me, do you?

SARAH
  Nah, should I.

VINCENT
  Never mind.

SARAH
  Say, I bet you could really tear up the dance floor, huh.

VINCENT
  No, no I don't, uh, dance.

SARAH
  Then what *do* you do, go to small town barn dances in the middle of winter reading books?

VINCENT
  I'm just, uh...visiting.

SARAH
Who, the librarian?

VINCENT
My folks, down by Cape Rich.

SARAH
You don't say. I got a farm near Mountain Lake myself.

VINCENT
They just cottage there. I'm from Toronto.

SARAH
City slicker, huh...you sure we met before?

Beat.

VINCENT
You used to sit on me when we were kids.

SARAH
Gee, you got...tall.

VINCENT
Uh, that your parent's farm you live on-

SARAH
My parents died a couple years ago.

VINCENT
Oh, uh, sorry to hear that.

SARAH
Just me now.

VINCENT
Live up there alone then?

The Tank Range Project

SARAH
Neighbors help out. You don't really know St. Vincent, do you?

VINCENT
Well enough. My dad needed help fishing so I-

SARAH
Fishing, in the winter?

VINCENT
Yeah, you never hear of ice fishing before?

SARAH
Sure, just never thought anyone actually did it.

VINCENT
How do you, uh, do it; the cold, the isolation? Would drive me nuts.

SARAH
Strength, courage...and a sniff of brandy.

The Conga song begins to play.

SARAH
What's your name city slicker?

VINCENT
Vincent...Vincent Whitelaw.

SARAH
Nice to meet you Vincent...Vincent Whitelaw. I'm Sarah...Sarah Vail.

VINCENT
You do the conga?

SARAH
The what?

VINCENT
Follow my lead...

He pulls her onto the dance floor.

SARAH
Thought you couldn't-

VINCENT
Put your hands here.

Vincent joins the conga line, Sarah getting the hang of it. They eventually break away.

VINCENT
Whoa!

SARAH
That was exhilarating. Knew you could dance city boy.

VINCENT
Well, I...that was fun.

They stare at one another for a long moment.

VINCENT
Wait a second, wait a second, this isn't right.

SARAH
What.

VINCENT
(Placing the book down in front of her)
Stand on this.

SARAH
What for.

The Tank Range Project

VINCENT
You'll see.

SARAH
I will, will I?

She stands on the book.

VINCENT
Close your eyes.

SARAH
Is this another one of your dancing tricks?

VINCENT
You'll see. Close your eyes, trust me.

She closes her eyes. Vincent puts her hands on his shoulders.

SARAH
I'm losing my balance-

Vincent kisses her.

SARAH
(breaking away)
I should go.

VINCENT
Valentine's night? You got another guy or something-

SARAH
No. Look, uh, Vincent, you're real nice but I...

VINCENT
Well spit it out, I'm real nice but what-

SARAH
But I never really, uh, kissed a boy without dating before. Why don't you call me sometime. Maybe we can read a book together or something.

VINCENT
(chuckling)
...Read a book, huh.

SARAH
Sure.

VINCENT
I got a better idea. Why don't we get out of here, take a turn around the lake, call it a date and go from there.

Beat.

SARAH
Ball of fire...

Vincent begins to leave.

VINCENT
...What do you say?

Sarah slowly follows. She finds the silver dollar and secretly pockets it, exiting with Vincent.

Blue Eyes notices the dollar is gone from her hand, when suddenly:

SCENE 2. "THE PITCH"

Brigadier General Robert Spencer appears, entering with a limp on one leg, a folder in hand. Blue Eyes watches.

SPENCER
Owning to unforeseen difficulties, the Armored Fighting Vehicle training range at Hawkstone near Lake Simcoe was not yet completed as initially planned. Upon inspection of the land, the Hawkstone range appeared to be

The Tank Range Project

sadly restricted both in breadth and depth with a target range of a mere 400 yards. It should be considered essential that tank crews learn what to expect under actual battle conditions, and at Hawkstone it is *im*possible within the present boundaries to simulate their roles efficiently.

Spencer opens the folder.

SPENCER
A recent report on an area north-west of Meaford, Ontario reveals approximately 17, 000 acres of land that appears to be highly suitable for tank training in every respect. It is adjacent to a good highway and the Canadian National Railway Line. It is sufficiently large enough to accommodate a range, and is adequately supplied with water from the Georgian Bay. It is comprised mainly of...farms and cottages in more or less poor condition. It is recommended that the entire rectangle be purchased so as to ensure that the training requirements of the present can be carried out in a satisfactory manner.

Spencer is approved. He marches off, Blue Eyes following.

Blue Eyes is stopped by a fallen apple.

SCENE 3. "THE PROPOSALS"

Carl, a farmer, reads over a pamphlet to Sarah on her porch.

Blue Eyes hovers nearby unseen, eating the apple.

CARL
"Welcome to St. Vincent Township! Your ticket to cottage country bliss! From the Irish Mountain views in the south, to the easterly escarpment along grand Georgian Bay, to old Cape Rich on the north-east tip, across to the western historic Vail's Point, down through meandering Sucker Creek, into the immovable Mountain Lake"-

SARAH
Immovable, oh I like that Carl.

CARL
Thank you Sarah. "The immovable...The Mountain Lake district is unique. It is located about nine miles from the town of Meaford, Ontario. Mountain Lake is 200 feet higher than Georgian Bay; well wooded, with excellent boating, bathing and fishing for both pickerel and bass. A most restful spot, with refreshing spring water and invigorating air!"

SARAH
Nice touch.

CARL
"No better Salmon or trout trolling grounds around...

Carl becomes passionate, like telling a ghost story.

CARL
...Mountain Lake was formerly an old Indian restin' spot, and legend has it that 1, 000 Indians were drowned in its icy bottomless waters by an aged crone's curse while the warriors were on the war path...

Resuming as before.

CARL
...It is historic and a delightful place for a holiday!" What do ya think?

SARAH
Might want to hold back on the Indian bit, Carl.

CARL
It's true.

SARAH
It's folklore.

CARL
So they say. I seen things on that lake Sarah, let me tell ya. Things I should not be discussin' in your presence. That's the God's truth.

The Tank Range Project

SARAH
You be ready to open end of the month?

CARL
That's the plan.

SARAH
Seems like only yesterday you started this little project, Carl.

CARL
Not so little anymore, eh. Ten years ago, sittin' along Sucker Creek with the boys, skippin' rocks along the banks. The idea stuck, and before you know it, I'm buildin' those log cabins right along the lake. Think people'll come?

SARAH
I'd rent one out in a heartbeat.

CARL
Thought you'd have a proper opinion. Been workin' on this darn welcome pamphlet all last week.

SARAH
Just ease on the Indian stuff.

CARL
Oh I guess your right. Suppose it could scare people away.

SARAH
Where you advertising?

CARL
Meaford Express, Owen Sound. Might need to hit Toronto.

SARAH
You *have* to hit Toronto, they're your biggest market, Carl.

CARL

Oh I know I know...just hate dealing with them cityiots is all. One step at a time Sarah.

SARAH

You get a look at my apple orchard out there?

CARL

Them blossoms are really takin' shape.

SARAH

About time, huh.

CARL

I'll say.

SARAH

Thanks for all your help Carl. I'll be getting those hired hands real soon, promise-

CARL

Sarah Vail, you stop right there, I won't hear nothin' of it, understan'. We have got to stick together through the good times and the bad, it's that simple.

Sarah nods acceptance.

CARL

Say, you think pink is too...froo froo for them cottages?

SARAH

Depends. What room?

CARL

Oh, for the bedrooms...and the kids' rooms...the kitchens, livin' rooms, porches...outhouse...pretty much the whole darn thing.

SARAH

Who told you to do that?

CARL
Wife. Says it's "all the craze" now.

SARAH
Pink? Really? I don't know.

CARL
Hm. Too late now, already on the final coat. Maybe I can at least redo the kitchens.

SARAH
Good luck with that.

CARL
Thanks for your help.

SARAH
See you tomorrow-

CARL
'morrow.

Carl leaves out back. Sarah goes inside her house.

Seeing that Sarah has gone inside, Vincent sneaks on. He carries a large picnic basket and a blanket over his arm. He stops, looks for the perfect spot to put it all down, and does so near a lilac tree.

He peeks inside the front window. Seeing Sarah, he quickly ducks down. He crawls back to the picnic.

He lays out the blanket stealthily and precise. He starts unpacking the picnic, staying low and watchful. First out is a large covered silver tray. He opens the lid, smelling a steaming breakfast, smiles, then covers it again, placing it precisely where it needs to be on the blanket.

VINCENT
(reciting)
"Look how this ring encompasseth thy..."

> *Suddenly the front door opens. Vincent quickly covers the picnic and himself with the blanket as best he can.*
>
> *Sarah steps outside placing a tray with a tea cup and saucer out onto the porch. She unassumingly goes back inside.*
>
> *Vincent uncovers himself. He takes Sarah's tray to the picnic. He sets back to his task, re-setting the blanket and all. He takes out cutlery and napkins, then a covered silver jam dish. He holds the dish for a beat, takes a deep breath, and sets it close by. He pulls out a bottle of brandy, takes a swig and puts it back into the basket. He plucks a flower from the lilac tree and sets it with the picnic. Straightening himself out, he takes a deep breath, reciting....*

VINCENT
"Look how this ring encompasseth thy finger, even so..."

> *Sarah comes outside with a teapot.*

VINCENT
Good morning Miss Vail.

SARAH
Miss Vail? After three months, you'd think we were past all the formalities. Good morning Mr. Whitelaw.

VINCENT
Good morning, Sarah. I, uh, I brought you breakfast.

SARAH
(seeing the picnic, sincere)
How thoughtful of you.

> *She sits at the picnic with the teapot.*

The Tank Range Project

SARAH
Thank you.

Vincent reaches for the teapot, cup and saucer.

VINCENT
Uh, how do you take your tea.

SARAH
Oh, just Red Rose.

VINCENT
No milk?

SARAH
Black.

VINCENT
Sugar?

SARAH
Nope.

VINCENT
Toast.

SARAH
No thanks.

Beat.

VINCENT
You...you sure you don't want some toast?

SARAH
Uh uh.

VINCENT
Well, uh, there's some jam to go with it, it's raspberry, fresh today.

SARAH
None for me.

Beat.

VINCENT
Not just, one slice?

SARAH
Mm mm.

Beat.

SARAH
Sit down Vincent, take a load off.

Vincent sits with her.

SARAH
Say, I finally read one of them Shakespeare books you told me about. What did you call it, um...um, King...

VINCENT
"King Lear".

SARAH
Yes, that's it. I couldn't sleep last night so I just read for a couple of hours.

VINCENT
I couldn't sleep either. I took a turn around Mountain Lake and down to Georgian Bay until the sun came up, trying to figure out our, uh, relationship.

SARAH
Have we got one of those?

VINCENT
Sure you won't have some toast and jam, at least just...

The Tank Range Project

He stands.

VINCENT
...open the lid!

She looks under the jam lid, seeing a ring box.

SARAH
You bought me a present.

VINCENT
"Look how this ring encompasseth thy finger, Even so thy breast encloseth my poor heart: wear both of them, for both of them are thine."

She opens the ring box.

Beat.

VINCENT
I hope it fits. I woke the postmaster at six o'clock this morning to pick it up.

SARAH
It's a lovely ring Vincent, really it is.

VINCENT
(sitting)
It's our, uh, engagement ring.

Beat.

SARAH
Vincent.

VINCENT
Well.

SARAH
You mean you...huh.

She takes out the ring, examining it closely.

VINCENT
What do you say?

SARAH
What do you want me to say?

VINCENT
Well just say yes, unless-

SARAH
Oh, Vincent...I think I better take a walk around the lake.

VINCENT
(nervous laughter)
I'm just as shocked as you. Marriage; I thought I was married to my books...but being around you these past few months...you see dust has been piling up on my heart; and it took you to blow it all away.

SARAH
Yeah but I...I didn't mean to blow it smack into your eyes.

VINCENT
Alas, that's what happened.

SARAH
Vincent I-

There is a rumble of thunder. Sarah looks up.

SARAH
What do you say we head inside.

VINCENT
Uh, okay but-

SARAH
I should really close those windows.

She goes inside, ring still in hand.

Vincent gathers up the picnic, taking a moment with the ring box. Setting it aside, he pulls out the brandy and swigs.

The storm continues rumbling closer. Spencer arrives.

SPENCER
Hell of a storm coming.

Vincent fumbles to put the brandy away, The ring box remaining out.

VINCENT
Huh?...oh, uh, yeah-

SPENCER
Little early, don't you think-

VINCENT
I know, I, uh, I was just, uh...testing it, uh...Cider, apple cider testing, uh...Can I help you?

SPENCER
Are you Mr. Vail?

VINCENT
Um...no.

SPENCER
Is Sarah Vail at home?

VINCENT
Inside. Why, who are you?

SPENCER
It's a personal matter.

Sarah enters.

SARAH
Vin, you'd better get in here, that storm is-

She sees Spencer.

SARAH
Oh, hello.

SPENCER
Sarah Vail?-

VINCENT
Can I help you sir?

SARAH
It's alright Vincent. What can I do for you mister?

VINCENT
I'm going to take another turn around the lake. Excuse me.

Vincent leaves.

SARAH
Vincent, take an umbrella at least!

SPENCER
Your boyfriend?

SARAH
...You could sort of say that.

SPENCER
You Sarah Vail?

SARAH
Sure am. What can I do for you Mister...?

SPENCER
Robert Spencer. I'm a surveyor. Mind if I step inside?

The Tank Range Project

SARAH
Got a card or something?

SPENCER
Here you go.

He hands her a card.

SARAH
Surveyor, huh. With the government.

SPENCER
That's right. Need to take a look around is all.

SARAH
(looking up at the storm)
Come in, come in.

They go inside.

SARAH
Let me take your coat.

SPENCER
That won't be necessary, won't be long. Beautiful tree you have out there.

SARAH
Lilac.

SPENCER
Smells nice.

SARAH
Got apples out back.

SPENCER
Must bring in a pretty penny.

SARAH
Sure oughta. Dad planted that orchard ten years ago, this is the first season it's actually yielding.

A loud thunder crack.

SARAH
One heck of a storm. That your car out there?

SPENCER
Company's.

SARAH
That so. Now what does a government survey company want with a girl like me?

SPENCER
It's about the road up this way-

SARAH
You're finally building a proper road up here?

SPENCER
Yes. You see, we just want to assess all the properties along its path for...well, there'll be some considerable construction these next coming months-

SARAH
They've been promising us that Bluewater Highway up here to Mountain Lake since last summer.

SPENCER
Mind if I take a quick tour of the house miss Vail?

SARAH
What, you building a road through my kitchen?

The Tank Range Project

SPENCER
(chuckling)
No, of course not. Just want to survey the property is all.

SARAH
My parents bought it for a good price back then. Bet that road will really bring some value to the land now, huh.

SPENCER
Might just. Mind if I...

SARAH
Sure sure, go ahead, take a look around.

SPENCER
Your parents still-

SARAH
Died a couple years back.

SPENCER
Sorry to hear that.

SARAH
Can I make you some tea?

SPENCER
No, thank you.

SARAH
This is great news Mister Spencer. I mean tourism alone...

SPENCER
It is gorgeous out here.

SARAH
Say, what happened to your leg?

SPENCER
War injury.

SARAH
This one or the last?

SPENCER
Last one.

SARAH
Think this one's going to end soon?

SPENCER
Hard to tell.

SARAH
I sure hope so.

SPENCER
Your boyfriend-

SARAH
He's not my boyfriend.

SPENCER
No?

SARAH
Nah, he's...

SPENCER
He enlisted?

SARAH
He'll be training at Hawkstone starting next week, heard of that? Some reason, he wants to leave his job to drive them fancy new gunner trucks-

SPENCER
M3 Ram Tanks.

The Tank Range Project

SARAH
Sure, that what you call them? Ugly looking things, you ask me.

SPENCER
Hawkstone, huh.

SARAH
You know the place?

SPENCER
Near Lake Simcoe.

SARAH
That's it. Vincent, well, he's a real scholarly type, likes reading them strategy books, and them Shakespeare histories, says he could really give this war a boost.

SPENCER
We need more men like him over there.

SARAH
You going back?

SPENCER
Not with my leg. Government work suits me just fine for now.

SARAH
You find what you're looking for here?

SPENCER
Yes, thank you. I'd better be on my way. Sorry to disturb you.

SARAH
Think nothing of it.

SPENCER
I'm sure we'll meet again.

Sarah walks Spencer out.

SARAH
Drive safe.

Spencer leaves. Sarah walks over to the lilac tree.

SARAH
They're building that road.

Sarah sees the ring box near the picnic spot. She takes the ring out of her pocket, puts it on and contemplates.

The storm begins raging. Sarah goes for cover under the porch.

Vincent returns. Sarah hides her ring finger.

VINCENT
Your friend leave?

SARAH
Never met him before.

VINCENT
Oh.

SARAH
He's gone. Vincent, you're wetter than a drowned kitten-

VINCENT
(reciting)
"May is the cruellest month, breeding
Lilacs out of the dead land, mixing
Memory and desire, stirring
Dull roots with spring rain."
Sarah Vail, I love you-

SARAH
-Vincent I-

VINCENT
-as much as you love this little piece of heaven-

SARAH
-I-

VINCENT
-I'm off next week and from there, who knows-

SARAH
That's just it Vin-

VINCENT
Sarah Vail, I want you to be that part that has been missing in my heart; from across Mountain Lake and back again.

She reveals her ring finger, and runs out to Vincent. They kiss passionately and escape inside.

SCENE 4. "THE SONG IS YOU"

The storm concludes abruptly. Blue Eyes remains, picking up the lilac flower. She puts on her headphones.

Spencer appears, handing out business cards to citizens.

Vincent and Sarah appear, being married.

Blue Eyes takes off the headphones.

SCENE 5. "CALL TO ARMS"

Vincent is atop a tank, speaking to his fellow soldiers.

VINCENT
Heroes; that is what we are. The reason we are here, entering the lion's den at last, is that we love what our country stands for. We are fighting in this other place, in the dirt, on that beach, and I am reminded of my own dirt and sand. I'm reminded that one day I will dip with my future son into

beautiful Georgian Bay. I will sit on the porch with my wife overlooking apple orchards and lilac landscapes, listening to a rainstorm sweep over our protected roof. And one day all this world will have a roof over their heads, because we few, we happy few, we made that happen. "Once more unto the breach, dear friends, once more; Or close the wall up with our English dead."

A soldier is heard from below.

SOLDIER
Lieutenant Vincent Whitelaw?

VINCENT
Yes.

SOLDIER
Been looking for you everywhere. Got a letter for you.

An enveloped letter is handed up to Vincent.

VINCENT
Bet it's from my wife. We got a hundred acre farm in St. Vincent Township, Ontario. Know the place?

SOLDIER
Nope.

VINCENT
You got any land?

No response.

VINCENT
Best thing you will ever do some day, mark my words. One thing they aren't making any more of.

Vincent reads the letter.

Pause.

The Tank Range Project

VINCENT
   They can't do that...

   A loud bullhorn blows.

VINCENT
   ...Can they?

   The tank engine roars. Vincent fades away. Blue Eyes is alone.

SCENE 6. "THE FACTS"

   Spencer speaks to the townsfolk. Blue Eyes listens.

SPENCER
...altogether, 100 farms in concessions 6 through 12, in all 17, 000 acres in St. Vincent Township have been designated to be expropriated within the next month by September 30th, 1942 the latest. Also to be expropriated are four schools, five churches, and two cemeteries, which includes 35 miles of shoreline property along Vail's Point, Cape Rich and Mountain Lake. Your land will be properly compensated for, and remember, the value of a soldier's life in Europe does not have a price, so we are compensating each farm according to a strict military budget, and rest assured that one day your land will likely be returned to you. While the war rages on however, we will utilize the surveyed land for ultimate training of the latest tank technologies, and your heroic patriotism just by allowing this to happen, will be documented for future generations to look upon with nationalistic pride. The tank range project should be...*will* be a symbol of heroism for the community of St. Vincent, we guarantee it!

   Spencer fades away.

SCENE 7. "TRANSFORMATION"

   1943. A Girl and a Boy climb from behind a fence. Blue Eyes watches them.

GIRL
   Over here.

Jamie Robinson & Roger Shank

BOY
Are we allowed?

GIRL
Ah, come on, don't chicken out now.

BOY
Okay okay.

GIRL
Climb the fence.

BOY
Where are we?

GIRL
It's my dad's old apple orchard, now come on!

BOY
I'm coming.

GIRL
Look at them clouds.

BOY
Bright red smoke clouds.

GIRL
Smelly here.

BOY
Like gasoline.

GIRL
I like gasoline.

BOY
You like gasoline, that's funny.

The Tank Range Project

GIRL
Just the smell, silly.

A muffled bomb is heard in the distance.

BOY
What's that sound!

GIRL
I don't know.

A soldier is heard from offstage.

SOLDIER
Hey you kids, get away from there!

GIRL
Quick, hide over here!

BOY
Wait for me!

They hide near Blue Eyes. The bombs get closer.

GIRL
Shh!

They both remain silent, alert and scared.

SOLDIER
Get out of there, now!

The Girl and Boy escape back over the fence, running off.

SCENE 8. "ONE WAY OR ANOTHER"

Spencer and Sarah are mid-conversation, Sarah tending her garden. Blue Eyes observes.

SPENCER
...One way or another we *will* be on your land-

SARAH
Oh look at you with your brass buttons and fancy hat-

SPENCER
-Sarah Whitelaw-

SARAH
-Thought you said you were surveying the place-

SPENCER
We *did* inform your husband of our intents.

SARAH
By what, by mail?

SPENCER
I assure you as I assured the others-

SARAH
How can you possibly assure us? There's a family two farms over, just finished filling a whole barn with hay last week, do it every season, and you tell them they got to be out of there by Monday? You probably don't know this, but a barn full of hay is worth at least a year's salary, and you don't just move a barn full of hay and a family with seven children in it over to a new home in less than a week.

SPENCER
Families overseas had even less time than that, believe me, and they were shot, killed if they didn't obey-

SARAH
Might as well shoot us too, what you want to pay us.

SPENCER
It is market value.

The Tank Range Project

SARAH
You're offering us less than what it was twenty years ago!

SPENCER
And the more you protest, the less you'll get. These are struggling economic times.

SARAH
May I remind you that not so long ago we struggled through the Depression and never asked anybody for a dollar all that time. Talk to them fishermen out on Vail's Point; ask them what the two hundred dollars you're paying them will do, and they'll say this is ten times worse than the Depression ever was.

SPENCER
I am simply doing my job, my duty. And you should too.

SARAH
You aren't even giving us a choice mister.

Carl enters.

SARAH
Seems there's no accounting for respecting anyone's place in this world anymore, is there.

SPENCER
Your property will be returned to you when this war is over.

SARAH
Hm.

CARL
Everything alright here Sarah?

SARAH
Carl, this is Brigadier Robert Spencer.

SPENCER
Brigadier *General*.

Sarah continues gardening.

SARAH
He's here to *assure* me-

CARL
Think I saw you walkin' through Meaford yesterday, that right? Suppose you're the one suggestin' we all take an early retirement from our premises, that right?

SPENCER
We certainly have been assessing the idea for sometime now.

CARL
Isn't that funny, because I been assessin' a thing or two myself these past few days and let me tell ya, that promise you made to us 'bout gettin' our homes back when this whole mess overseas is cleared up-

SPENCER
Not necessarily a promise-

CARL
Well let's just hope it holds water, because as much as we understand our *patriotic duty*, you need to assess what a community several generations along means to the true value of this land.

SPENCER
We are making our best efforts to work with the community-

Spencer begins to itch.

CARL
You never knew my dad. Or his dad even, or the families who came before him. My dad grew up on a farm between Mountain lake and Sucker Creek, know where that is?

The Tank Range Project

SPENCER
Uh...

Spencer itches more.

CARL
The land was mostly clay and shale rock back then, but the people farmed it. You wanna know anythin' 'bout this area, ask someone who grew up here. They'll tell ya every inch and detail about it.

Sarah stops gardening.

SARAH
Something a matter there, Brigadier *General*?

SPENCER
No, no I'm fine, just, uh...mosquito bites.

CARL
How'd you get over here?

SPENCER
Drove through the trail there-

CARL
Go along a slopin' ravine?

SPENCER
Yes. I got turned around at a cave.

CARL
Did you get outta the vehicle 'long that path?

SPENCER
Just to, uh...to pee.

CARL
You thinkin' what I'm thinkin' Sarah?

SARAH
Hog's Back Trail?

SPENCER
What?

> *Carl and Sarah look to each other. Spencer looks at them desperately, itching.*

SPENCER
Look, I have a whole day of farms to see yet-

CARL
Well you'd better hop on to it, hadn't you Brigadier General Spencer.

SPENCER
(to Sarah)
We'll be using your kitchen as a-

SARAH
I know I know, as the main headquarters or whatever the heck you call it-

SPENCER
-barracks for the compound-

CARL
Barracks. Whatever. Now get off her damn property, you're still trespassin'.

> *Spencer begins to leave, itching excruciatingly.*

SPENCER
It is technically Crown land Mrs. Whitelaw-

CARL
Oh go on with ya.

> *Spencer leaves, still itching.*

SARAH
"Leaves of three, let them be."

CARL
He'll be at that for hours.

SARAH
We could have told him the remedy I suppose.

CARL
Nah.

Beat.

CARL
Think we'll get our farms back Sarah?

SARAH
Who know's Carl. Government has power. And depending how long this war goes...

CARL
I'll at least get my cabins back, right? Been rentin' out like crazy all summer.

SARAH
How much time they give *you*?

CARL
End o' September. Same as most everyone else.

SARAH
Some gone already.

CARL
Bill lost seventy-five tonnes o' crop, couldn't move it in time.

SARAH
Shame that.

CARL
What gets me Sarah, is the cause they say we're supposed to be supportin'. Like I told my boys before they shipped out, you're not fightin' for home or the flag or for all that crap, you're fightin' for each other, just for each other. Not gonna let my three come home to nothin'; after what they're goin' through? Doesn't seem right.

SARAH
Your boys are real heroes.

CARL
Hear from Vincent?

Beat.

SARAH
Not in a while.

CARL
He's a good husband Sarah, 'member him as a kid. Smart as a whip. I'm sure he'll come in handy on the battlefield, you mark my words.

SARAH
Thanks Carl, I need to hear that. No one around here seems to talk much about the happenings over there.

CARL
His *real* trainin' will come on the battlefield. No need for another military base, 'specially 'round here.

SARAH
Suppose your right.

CARL
Oh jeese, the reason I come over, almost forgot.

SARAH
What's that?

The Tank Range Project

CARL
I'm havin' a meetin' at my barn Tuesday night, all the township's gonna be there if they can. Gonna discuss how we might make this little problem go away.

SARAH
I'll be there.

CARL
Everyone's on our side Sarah, we can beat this thing. Wife's makin' her famous apple pie, I know you love.

SARAH
You know I do. Say, you ever paint over that pink?

CARL
You kiddin'. I complained 'bout it to the wife and she just looks at me says, "Frankly my dear, I don't give a damn!" She's been goin' to them picture shows with her girlfriends too much, what I think.

SARAH
But the cottages still rent out?

CARL
Yes. I suppose she has wive's intuition or some such thing. Every *guy* looks 'round the place in disbelief, while the wife screams, "Oh, how wonderful! The pink is so delightful, isn't it honey!" Can barely see that fresh cedar brown through the damn froo froo pink no more, ruined the whole darn thing, you ask me.

SARAH
I really oughta see them sometime.

CARL
Well I'll see you Tuesday night. Come a little early and I'll give ya the grand tour.

SARAH
What time?

CARL
Five o'clock sound okay?

SARAH
Perfect.

CARL
Maybe we should invite Brigadier General Spencer along.

SARAH
I don't think he'll want anything to do with us once that ivy rash clears up.

CARL
Poor guy. The army has no idea what kind of mud they're churnin' up here, do they.

SARAH
Sure don't Carl.

CARL
(saluting)
See you Tuesday then, at seventeen-hundred hours Sergeant.

SARAH
See you then.

Carl exits..

SCENE 9. "TRIO"

Sarah puts down her gardening, caresses her belly and goes to the lilac tree. Vincent appears, continuing as he was last seen.

SARAH
August never felt so cold.

Sarah exits into her house.

The Tank Range Project

> *A headlight suddenly flashes on Blue Eyes. Explosion. Blue Eyes hangs over the turret.*

SCENE 10 "GOD?"

> *Vincent is mid-battle inside his tank. He talks on a military radio headset.*

VINCENT
...Our loader's been shot dead! My periscope's blown out!...Snipers!...I can't hear...no I know we're in the wrong place, that's what I'm trying to tell you Sergeant, our coordinates are all wrong!...We're killing civilians!...Damn it! Radio's dead!

> *Vincent yells below.*

VINCENT
Aim higher, aim higher! Up 200 yards, angle 400 left!

> *A big explosion. Vincent is hit, hanging over the turret. Injured, he crawls off the tank.*

VINCENT
(praying)
Our father, who art in heaven, hallowed be thy name...

> *Blue Eyes comes to, hearing Vincent's prayer. She approaches him.*

VINCENT
God!?

BLUE EYES
Come with me.

VINCENT
Who are you?

BLUE EYES
Follow me. You'll be safe.

The barrage of shelling re-ignites, intensifying. Vincent is suddenly dragged away.

VINCENT
No!

BLUE EYES
Vincent!

The Tank Range Project

On Mountain Lake.

Lugging the Bayview Baptist Church off the land.

The Tanks Rolled In.

The Tank Range Project

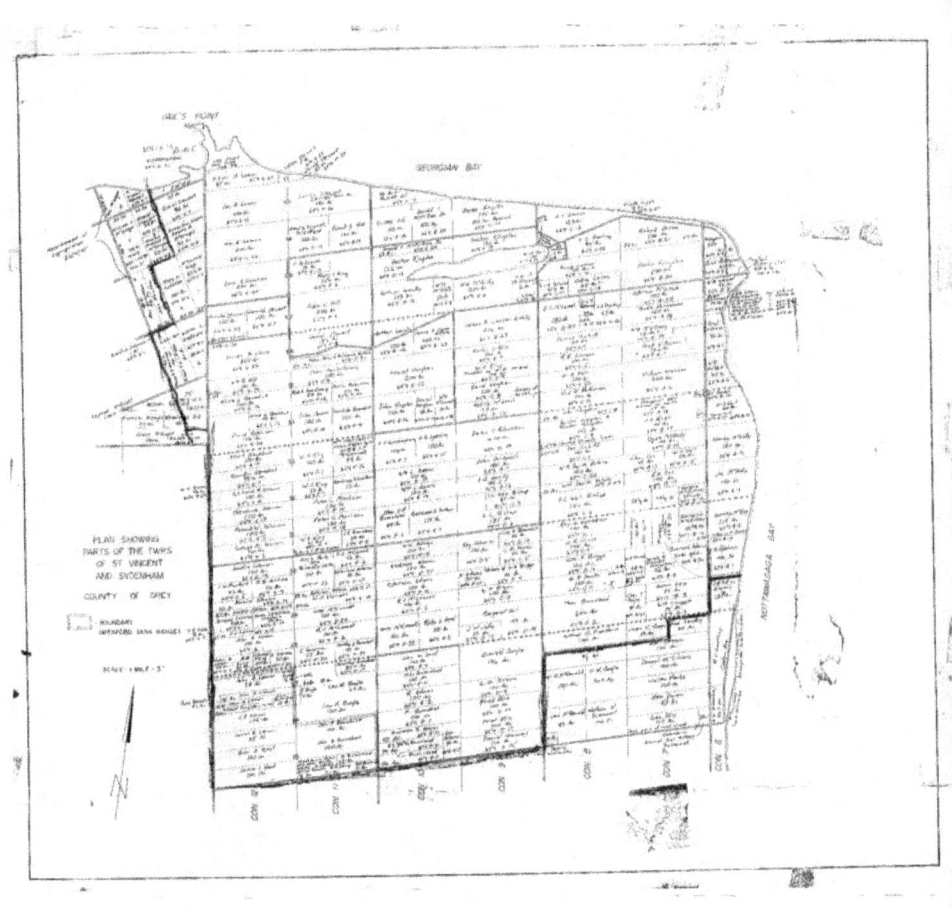

Map of the Expropriated Area 17,000 Acres.

Jamie Robinson & Roger Shank

SCENE 11. "FARM AUCTION"

The house lights come up to full as an Auctioneer addresses the audience, speaking at a traditional farm auctioneers' pace. Blue Eyes watches.

AUCTIONEER
...2 cows dairy cows good for milkin' good for breedin', easy cream cheque every month, 2 cows going once, going twice...sold to number 989, that you Mel?...number 989. Next up, a canoe old canoe the one John Vail arrived in up at Vail's point in 1825, the year Meaford got it's start...start the bidding at 5 dollar 5 dollar anyone 5 dollar...I hear 10, 10, 10...15...15 over there 15, 15, 15...20, 20, 20 I hear, 25...25, 25, 25, any 30...25 going once 25 going twice 25, 25...sold to number 156. Number 156, looks like Doris and Leda, beautiful pair a' women but a little backward you ask me...next an old saw taken from the Carson House Saw Mill, originally the Doran home built back some 100 years ago in 1836, now to be demolished over by a good ol' Canadian Ram Tank...1 dollar 1 dollar 1, 1, 1...2 dollars 2, 2, there's 2 do I see 3 dollars...5 there's 5, 5, 5...6 dollars?...5 going once going twice...sold for 5 dollars, number 282, Mr. Gowdy, number 282. Up next a pair a' mittens...torn up mittens worn by Mr. Carson last winter when he was found frozen to death, trying to follow the barbed wire fence home, trying to find his way out of the field one stormy winter night...historic mittens torn to shreds.

Beat.

AUCTIONEER
Moving right along...Next up, 1, 7000 acres of prime farming, orchard, milling, fishing, topsoil LAND...never owned by the farmers living there, never owned by the slaves that escaped there, never owned by the Indians who passed through there, but suddenly owned by the King who's never even been there...SOLD FOR THE PRICE OF 3 RAM TANKS BY THE MINISTRY OF DEFENCE COMING DOWN THE OLD MAIL ROAD, RE-WRITING OUR HISTORY FOREVER!...SOLD SOLD SOLD!!!

He fades away as Blue Eyes looks up and the house lights go out.

The Tank Range Project

SCENE 12. "THINK TANK"

Sarah is mid-conversation with Carl. Blue Eyes hovers nearby.

CARL
...This is not good Sarah, not good at all.

SARAH
Carl, we can't give up on this yet, you hear.

CARL
You heard what Bill was sayin' in there, they practically gave him nothin' for his farm; $4, 300 for a hundred acres? It's worth at least ten thousand. What the hell they gonna offer us?

SARAH
I know.

CARL
Mel over on 7th line, had to move 22 head o' cattle 15 miles to his new home on 9th line...*in a day*? On property half the size, costin' *twice* as much as the government paid for his.

SARAH
I think the petition idea is a great start, Carl.

CARL
Sure, some idea that was. Whole community's scared by big bully government. I was on my own in there Sarah.

SARAH
We can get those signatures in a couple days.

CARL
Won't be fast enough the way they're goin' at it. I thought the auctioneer was fast, but these guys...well they got us caught in a sling. Hay sellin' for $1 a tonne? It's robbery! And I just sunk everythin' I got into them cedar cabins. Never had debt in my life, but at this rate...

SARAH
 Carl-

CARL
 Who really owns the land we harvest Sarah, the water we drink? Look at that lake. So many stories, and for what? Men coming home to nothin'.

SARAH
 Carl, we need your strength.

CARL
 Not much left, Sarah. Wife's hangin' by a thread. Haven't heard from the boys in weeks. It ain't like them at all.

SARAH
 Been a lot of Canadian action this summer, I know. We have to be strong for them.

CARL
 You want kids some day?

SARAH
 Of course.

CARL
 Maybe you...ought to move on?

SARAH
 What?

CARL
 I've lived, Sarah, had a real nice life, built my dream cottages, made a few people happy, and I am gonna stick this situation out, you hear, right to the end. But you and a lot of these young folk...I mean maybe we're just in the wrong place at the wrong time-

SARAH
 -Carl-

The Tank Range Project

CARL
-No no, I mean it Sarah. Strange things go on 'round here. Maybe we should just look at it all from a different angle, see.

SARAH
We'll get the petition started and take it from there. There has to be a way.

CARL
Suppose so. Best get back inside to the wife.

SARAH
Thank her for the pie. It was a real, "Killer Diller".

CARL
Can you believe she said that? "Killer Diller", describin' a pie. Too many picture shows.

SARAH
Goodnight Carl. Your cottages are beautiful, they really are...even with the pink.

CARL
Good night Sarah.

Sarah leaves. Carl looks across the lake.

CARL
17, 000 acres for the price of three Ram Tanks. 17, 000 acres for the price of three Ram Tanks!

Carl turns to go inside, stops and faces Blue Eyes. Blue Eyes faces Carl. They stare at one another for a time.

CARL
I'm countin' on you Mountain Lake. Don't wanna end up bein' folklore, you hear.

Carl goes indoors. Blue Eyes follows, but stops, turning to see:

SCENE 13. "CAPTIVITY"

Vincent in prison.

VINCENT
(reciting)
"Thoughts tending to ambition, they do plot
Unlikely wonders-

BLUE EYES
-Alive-

VINCENT
-how these vain weak nails..."

Blue Eyes goes to Vincent.

VINCENT
Sarah?

BLUE EYES
No. We're alive.

VINCENT
"...May tear a passage through-

BLUE EYES
-Someone's coming-

VINCENT
-the flinty ribs-

BLUE EYES
-do what they say-

VINCENT
-of this hard world-

The Tank Range Project

BLUE EYES
-and always remember Sarah-

VINCENT
-my ragged prison walls"-

BLUE EYES
It's going to be alright. Remember Sarah.

SCENE 14. "M.I.A."

Sarah sits inside her house sipping tea, as soldiers mill about preparing their barracks. Blue Eyes watches her.

SARAH
(to a soldier)
Need a hand.

She claps unenthusiastically. She goes to use the phone, picks up the receiver and listens to the empty sound.

SARAH
Damn it!

Sarah slams the phone down and follows the chord, finding it unplugged, a military radio replacing the wiring.

A soldier stomps through.

SARAH
Oh don't worry, I'll sweep that up in a minute. Hooligans!

A soldier hands a black-etched telegram to Sarah. She opens it and reads.

Soldiers continue milling around Sarah. She confronts a soldier.

SARAH
Where's the Brigadier General?

Jamie Robinson & Roger Shank

The soldier points. Sarah runs out.

SCENE 15. "PAINT JOB"

Carl appears with a can of paint. Blue Eyes follows as he fades away.

SCENE 16. "TIME"

Blue Eyes sees Vincent.

BLUE EYES
Vincent.

VINCENT
Huh...

BLUE EYES
Vincent, wake up.

VINCENT
Sarah.

BLUE EYES
Listen to me.

VINCENT
Who are you? Am I dead?

BLUE EYES
I...I don't think so.

Beat.

BLUE EYES
I think I'm an angel. I think I'm *your* angel and I'm here to protect you, you understand?

VINCENT
I don't believe in angels.

BLUE EYES
Neither do I. Your wife-

Spencer and Sarah appear atop a windmill.

VINCENT
Sarah! You've seen Sarah?

BLUE EYES
Yes.

SCENE 17. "WINDMILL"

Blue Eyes and Vincent see Spencer and Sarah and watch from below.

SPENCER
...This windmill is the perfect place to survey from. You see that over there, that little peak cresting in the distance?

SARAH
(bland)
Vinegar Hill. Local farmers just hauled the Bayview Baptist Church from there last week; seven teams of horses and a tractor, through two miles of swamp.

SPENCER
You see that regiment reaching the rising ground?

SARAH
Look like little ants-

SPENCER
There! Watch the sky fill up with machine gun tracer bullets.

They watch.

SPENCER
That's thousands of bullets screaming through the air pouring into enemy defenses.

SARAH
Hard to believe we used to play hide & seek there-

SPENCER
Look at the volume and accuracy that these troops can produce already-

Vincent is unheard by Sarah and Spencer.

VINCENT
Big elm trees, easy to climb, never found until dark-

SPENCER
Two inch mortar from within every tank finishing the scenario-

SARAH
Run home to fresh apple, peach, or raspberry pie-

SPENCER
laying a thick red smoke screen on the surface so tanks can ferret away to safety.

SARAH
One thing they're not making any more of...

SARAH, VINCENT & BLUE EYES
...Land.

SPENCER
Why? Why do you people need this land so much, when our boys are over there, miles and miles away, fighting for our freedom, on someone else's land, dying to protect us from the enemy?

SARAH
Our roots run deep in this area.

SPENCER
You got that telegram about your husband?-

SARAH
Don't! Please.

SPENCER
From up here, thirty feet in the air, windmill swishing around so peaceful, I know that I want all my land and country to stay this calm. Imagine we didn't find this. Imagine how quickly that beautiful shoreline would get eaten up by developers and city venturers. You would lose this calm for good. Such perfect terrain for our tanks; the rolling hills, the valleys, the plains, the lake...Your husband-

SARAH
-Don't!-

SPENCER
-If he'd had proper training like this-

SARAH
I don't believe that.

VINCENT
Believe Sarah.

SPENCER
He's just M.I.A.

SARAH
Just M.I.A.?

SPENCER
Lots go Missing In Action are found again. There's hope.

SARAH
Hope is just...

VINCENT
...as faded as them autumn apple trees.

SARAH
...as useless as them torn up petition papers. You say we may get our land back someday after this war is over, for what!? So kids can play with land mines and grenades, fiddling with old bombs buried in sand castles.

Vincent reaches up to Sarah. She winces in discomfort.

SARAH
...I'm dizzy.

Spencer holds her.

SPENCER
Don't look down.

She let's him hold her for a beat. Vincent releases his reach. Spencer let's go of Sarah.

SPENCER
Close your eyes.

SARAH
What for?

SPENCER & VINCENT
Trust me.

Sarah closes her eyes.

SPENCER
Imagine all that you just saw, in your mind's eye. Turn that into dugouts and ditches and battlegrounds and overturned tanks. Keep your eyes closed and imagine all that land, from Mountain Lake to Vail's Point, imagine all that in a war zone. Now open your eyes.

SARAH
I don't see your point.

The Tank Range Project

SPENCER
Sometimes you have to open your eyes to things you never saw before. This here is one part of our country. Overseas, they'll be cleaning up this kind of beauty for years to come. If there's no range, no one'll ever talk about this place. The sacrifice that you and your people are making will go down in history and you will be heroes, and that kind of beauty is priceless.

SARAH
You got us all figured out, don't you.

SPENCER
It's for the best-

SARAH
Just uproot a town and move right along.

SPENCER
Think of the lives your sacrifice will save.

SARAH
This land...

VINCENT
...this precious dirt and soil...

SARAH
...it was never guaranteed.

VINCENT
Seems the weeds have finally taken root.

SARAH
Time to find a new path...

VINCENT
...surrounded by apple orchards and yellow-capped fields.

SARAH
I suppose I don't think this way, I'll break into a thousand pieces.

SPENCER
I understand.

SARAH
How can you possibly understand? I'm going to go home; or to what's left of it.

SPENCER
I'll help you down.

They descend. A bomb goes off in the distance.

SARAH
Won't ever get used to that.

Another bomb.

SPENCER
Can I give you a ride home?

SARAH
I'll walk.

SPENCER
Watch out for poison ivy.

They leave opposite each other.

VINCENT
Sarah!

Another bomb.

BLUE EYES
She can't.

The Tank Range Project

Another several bombs in a row.

VINCENT
Sarah, no! Wait! Sarah, please, I need you.

SCENE 18. "SMOKE BOMB"

The Girl and Boy emerge, picking up and tossing a small object back and forth. Vincent and Blue Eyes watch.

GIRL
You catch!

BOY
Now you catch!

GIRL
Hot potato!

BOY
Boiling potato!

GIRL
Mashed potato!

BOY
Fried potato!

GIRL
Scallop potato!

The object begins to smoke in the Boy's hands.

BOY
Smoking potato?

GIRL
That's funny. You said smoking potato!

BOY
No, look. It's smoking.

GIRL
Golly. It is.

BOY
I bet it's a smoke bomb!

GIRL
Wow! Neat.

BOY
What was a smoke bomb doing in your daddy's apple orchard?

GIRL
I don't know. They said we could go back there to pick apples all day if we want.

BOY
We have a souvenir! Wow!

It stops smoking. The bomb goes off. The Girl, Boy and Blue Eyes fall to its explosion. Blue Eyes is separated from the kids and lands in Vincent's cell.

SCENE 19. "ESCAPE"

Vincent in his cell, recites to himself.

VINCENT
"Friends, Romans, countrymen, lend me your ears."

BLUE EYES
Hail Mary, full of grace the Lord is with Thee.

VINCENT
"Ask for me tomorrow, and you shall find me a grave man."-

BLUE EYES
-Blessed art Thou among women, and blessed is the fruit of Thy womb-

VINCENT
-"Mine honour is my life."-

Vincent attempts an escape. German voices are heard from offstage.

GERMAN VOICES
-Halten Sie, die gefangenen! (*Stop that prisoner!*)-

BLUE EYES
-Jesus-

VINCENT
-"Cowards die many times before their deaths."-

GERMAN VOICES
-Halten Sie jetzt! Jetzt, oder ich schiesse! (*Stop now! Now or I'll shoot!*)-

BLUE EYES
-Holy Mary, Mother of God, pray for us sinners-

VINCENT
-"The valiant never taste of death but once"-

GERMAN VOICES
-Tun, oder ich schiebe, verdammt! (*Do it, or I will shoot, damn it!*)-

BLUE EYES
-Now and in the hour of our death-

GERMAN VOICES
-Kannst Du mich verstehen! Halt! Jetzt! (*Do you understand me? Stop! Now!*)-

VINCENT
-"Cry 'Havoc,' and let slip the dogs of war."-

Vincent runs off to escape.

GERMAN VOICES
Eins! Zwei! Drei! (*One! Two! Three!*)

SCENE 20. "SACRIFICE"

Sarah appears, seeing a stump where the lilac tree used to be.

Blue Eyes watches as Spencer enters.

SARAH
(confronting Spencer)
Why...this tree?

SPENCER
We need the space to train our-

SARAH
-You good for nothing-

SPENCER
-These are difficult times-

SARAH
-heartless, deceitful-

SPENCER
-War is not easy-

SARAH
The highway you never built was to go right up to that tree, fixing the road that...you coward, you don't know the sacrifices my folks made-

SPENCER
You don't know sacrifice!

SARAH
I'm living it-

SPENCER
Ever been to battle?

SARAH
Of course not-

SPENCER
Ever trudged through a ten foot trench, rain hasn't stopped pouring for weeks-

SARAH
I've heard-

SPENCER
What have you heard? Hear the one about charging a useless front, driving a tank you never trained in before, firing away with brand new equipment, no idea how the hell to use it!

Beat.

Spencer stares at the unseen Blue Eyes. Sarah keeps her gaze on Spencer.

SPENCER
Bombed out terrain making it impassable for our shit hot tanks to get through. Our tank finally goes phut, she's lost a track, starts to sink, engine kaput; we get hit by a shell we'll be cooked alive. My partner, the big gunner, he won't quit. He evacuates from our protector, determined to get the track back on again. Ack-ack firing, Godamn him, that gunner works under the tank track like a brass hat. Pipsqueak me, crew commander, sitting inside with cold feet, just waiting to die. Gunner calls out to me, "Spencer"! I stumble out the hatch, lost out of my Goddamn mind. His big hands grab me out of nowhere, tells me to put a sock in it. We're going to use a thick plank to get that track back on its wheels. He's wedging the thing while I'm holding it, wading in blood and guts. He hops into the tank, somehow gets the engine rolling again. I'm still holding hard, needing a full revolution of the wheels to get things back on track. I'm losing my grip. I shout out, "Help! Help!" Big gunner jumps out to see me struggling. I hear the crunch of heavy machinery about to roll on top

of me. He takes the wedge with one hand, and with the other, grabs my free arm, pulling, pulling, pulling, just keeps pulling. I don't see that it's *him* taking on the increasing tonnage, and it's *him* pulling me out in the nick of time. It's him I'm staring at now...I quickly grab what arm of his is left to seize and give it all I've got. Big gunner just smiles that mysterious, beautiful smile that always kept our regiment at ease, and sinks, sinks, sinks, until all I can see are those eyes: those deep blue eyes peering through my soul. His hand slips from mine at last.

Spencer turns to Sarah.

SPENCER
How can I ever go back to that? How can I let our men go back...to that? The tanks will roll in here, and our men will be properly trained, I guarantee that much.

Spencer offers Sarah a contract to sign.

SPENCER
Your husband deserved that training.

Spencer leaves the contract behind and limps away.

Sarah holds the contract.

SARAH
I'm sorry Vincent.

An explosion.

SARAH
Our home.

She fades away.

SCENE 21. "PINK"

Carl is near a tank. Brush and can with him, he begins painting the tank pink.

The Tank Range Project

CARL
Welcome to St. Vincent Township! From the Irish Mountain views in the south, to the easterly escarpment along grand Georgian Bay. From old Cape Rich to historic Vail's Point, down through meandering Sucker Creek, into the immovable...the immovable Mountain Lake. The Mountain Lake district is unique. It is located about nine miles from the town of Meaford, Ontario, running east to west along the northern St. Vincent edge.

A soldier is heard from offstage.

SOLDIER
Hey mister! You are trespassing on military soil! You must leave the premises immediately, do you understand!-

CARL
I will not surrender what is rightfully mine-

SOLDIER
-Do you understand me!-

CARL
-This is my land, my farm!-

SOLDIER
-We're here to help you!-

CARL
-I will die for it-

SOLDIER
-We are on your side!

Carl takes out a contract and burns it.

SOLDIER
-I am giving you five seconds pal! One-

CARL
-I have a right to stay here-

SOLDIER
-Two-

CARL
-where three generations have stayed before me-

SOLDIER
-Three-

CARL
-You should surrender for trespassin' on my property!-

SOLDIER
-Four-

CARL
A most restful spot, with refreshing spring water and invigorating air.

SCENE 22. "CLEANSING"

Blue Eyes begins folding up the Concertainer unit.

Sarah appears, now in her nineties.

BLUE EYES
I'm sorry ma'am, are you supposed to be here?

SARAH
Visitor's day.

BLUE EYES
Of course.

Blue Eyes continues working as Sarah approaches a new lilac tree where the stump used to be.

The Tank Range Project

SARAH
Beautiful.

BLUE EYES
You know this place?

SARAH
Mountain Lake, sure do. I had a farm, right on that very spot. Watched it get blown away. Haven't been back since.

Beat.

BLUE EYES
(saluting Sarah)
It's an honour to meet you ma'am.

SARAH
What's your unit?

BLUE EYES
2nd Division, Canadian Infantry Brigade, battalion commander.

SARAH
My husband was in the same division, Second World War. Where were you deployed?

BLUE EYES
Used to be in Afghanistan before I...

Pause.

BLUE EYES
It's an honour.

As Blue Eyes finishes her work, she notices an old book.

BLUE EYES
Look at this.

Blue Eyes hands Sarah the book.

SARAH
Vincent!

Blue Eyes leaves.

EPILOGUE.

1942. Vincent enters, sneaking up on Sarah as she reads.

VINCENT
(frightening Sarah)
Mrs. Whitelaw.

SARAH
Ahh! Mr. Whitelaw. Husband.

VINCENT
Wife.

Sarah wrestles him to the ground, sitting on him.

SARAH
This what I used to do to you when we were kids?

VINCENT
Pretty darn close.

SARAH
Don't try and escape-

VINCENT
Sure-

SARAH
-or I'll-

The Tank Range Project

VINCENT
What-

SARAH
I'll tickle you.

She tickles him, but he remains serious.

SARAH
Ah come on, where's your sense of humour bookworm, floating down the creek or something.

VINCENT
Fish must have snagged it.

SARAH
What fish, there's no fish in that thing.

VINCENT
Old Sucker Creek, are you kidding me.

SARAH
Not a one, hardly any water.

VINCENT
You serious?

SARAH
That little stream, no fish swimming in there.

VINCENT
How much you want to bet.

SARAH
How are you going to prove it, got a rod?

VINCENT
How much?

SARAH
Tell you what, you catch a fish in there before sun down and I'll give you a whole dollar, how about that.

VINCENT
A whole dollar, huh. You got one on you?

SARAH
Mm hm, what do you say?

VINCENT
I got until sundown.

SARAH
That's right.

VINCENT
I'll catch one in less than a minute.

SARAH
Gee, you know something I don't?

VINCENT
A whole dollar remember.

SARAH
I gotta see this.

Sarah follows him to the creek. Vincent patiently awaits his moment.

VINCENT
(to the fish)
Here little fishy-

He reaches his hand down fast and pulls out a large fish, startling Sarah.

SARAH
Oh!-

VINCENT
-You stole my sense of humour fishy. Give it back or Sarah Whitelaw's going to eat you for dinner-

SARAH
-Put it back put it back, you're killing it-

VINCENT
(to Sarah)
Ah, she's fine, just a little shell shocked s'all-

SARAH
Vincent put it back, it's all wiggly-

VINCENT
Okay little fishy, in you go. Thanks for giving back my sense of humour.

Vincent puts the fish back in.

VINCENT
One dollar please.

SARAH
How did you do that?

VINCENT
Limestone bottom like that, ideal for spawning beds. Used to do it as kids all the time.

SARAH
Been here all my life and I never-

VINCENT
Sometimes you have to open your eyes to things you never seen before, who knows what you'll find in your own backyard.

SARAH
Like this dollar.

Sarah takes out the dollar coin and hands it to him.

VINCENT
That...

SARAH
...Yep-

VINCENT
My dollar-

SARAH
Didn't know if I'd actually see you after that Valentine's dance.

VINCENT
How did you-

SARAH
You getting sentimental over a dollar.

VINCENT
No, this dollar...My father gave it to me when I was fourteen years old. Was my first pay ever when I used to fish with him in the summers. He said to me, "Vincent, take this dollar and save it. One day you'll buy land of your own with it."

SARAH
What do you know. Now look at you, just bought a hundred acres of prime farm real estate in marrying me mister. Maybe I should take that dollar back.

VINCENT
(pocketing the dollar)
I bought a whole lot more than that.

They kiss.

SARAH
Did we really do this Vincent? Really really?

The Tank Range Project

VINCENT
From the top of Irish Mountain to the sunset at Mountain Lake, I hereby declare us officially married.

SARAH
Happened in a flash.

VINCENT
I know.

> *They hold each other silent for a time. Vincent notices something above.*

VINCENT
Look.

SARAH
What is it?

VINCENT
It's a-

VINCENT
(making sure)
...an eagle.

SARAH
This low?

VINCENT
Nesting.

SARAH
Watching.

> *Watching the eagle in bliss, Sarah and Vincent fade away with the setting sun. Sinatra plays softly.*

FIN.

ABOUT THE AUTHORS

JAMIE ROBINSON

Jamie is the co-founder/co-Artistic Director of The Grey-Bruce Arts Collective, co-writer of *The Tank Range Project*, head writer for several one-night original murder mystery creations for the Grey-Bruce region of Southwestern Ontario and collaborator for the collectives, *Beyond The Farm Show* (Blyth Festival) *The Rochdale Project* (Theatre Passe Muraille) and *The Rediscovery Of Sex* (Alianak Productions). Jamie's selected theatre acting credits include: Four seasons with The Stratford Festival of Canada including major roles in; *Edward II* (Gaveston), *Troilus & Cressida* (Achilles), and *Merchant Of Venice* (Prince Of Morocco); Title role in *Richard III* (Metachroma Theatre), *Gas Girls* (New Harlem Productions. Dora Award Nomination, Best Actor), *Angels In America* Parts I And II (Winnipeg Jewish Theatre), *Romeo & Juliet* (Canadian Stage in High Park), *The Incredible Speediness of Jamie Cavanaugh* (Roseneath Theatre U.S./Canada Tour), *The Last Days of Judas Iscariot* (Birdland Theatre), *Medea* (Mirvish/MTC), *Escape From Happiness* (Factory Theatre), *El Numero Uno, Touch The Sky, The Other Side Of The Closet* and *Anne* (Young People's Theatre). Film/TV acting credits include: *Murdoch Mysteries* (Shaftesbury), *The Rick Mercer Report* (CBC), *Against The Wall* (NBC), *Celeste In The City* (ABC), *'Twas The Night Before Christmas* (Disney), *The Fraternity* (Universal Studios) and *Kevin Hill* (CBS). Jamie is the recipient of two Stratford Guthrie Awards and is the co-founder of Montreal's Metachroma Theatre. He has taught as a Guest Artist for several Ontario Elementary and Secondary School Drama along with Shakespeare classes. Jamie is a graduate of The Stratford Birmingham Conservatory and holds a B.F.A. from Concordia University. He is currently an M.F.A. Candidate in York University's Theatre Director's Program.

www.jamierobinson.ca

The Tank Range Project

ROGER SHANK

B.F.A. In Acting from the University of Alberta (Dean's List). Artistic Director of the Grey-Bruce Arts Collective and co-author of The Tank Range Project. He has directed three plays for The 100 Mile Playwright Festival; Beautiful Joe, The Tank Range Project and Spring Time. Roger directed The Good Soul of Szechuan for the Huron Epic Youth at the Blyth Festival. Roger is the creator and co-director of the innovative youth film program, MY (Meaford Youth) Film Studio. As a professional instructor, Roger teaches theatre arts at St. Clair College in Windsor, Ontario where he recently directed a production of Michael O'Brien's Gods Wounds. Acting credits include: Constable Howard and Ensemble (The Donnelly's: Sticks & Stones), Sir Thomas Berkeley (Edward II), Diomedes (Troilus and Cressida), Menecrates (Antony and Cleopatra), Joseph (The Taming of the Shrew), Jehan (The Hunchback of Notre Dame), Sir Andrew foulkes (The Scarlet Pimpernel), Dumaine (All's Well That Ends Well), Edmund's Knight (King Lear) for the Stratford Festival. Selected theatre credits: Brick, Cat on a Hot Tin Roof (Neptune Theatre); William Roper, A Man for All Seasons (Citadel Theatre, directed by Robin Phillips); Lt. Dancock, Dancock's Dance, and Lee, Melville Boys (Theatre North West); Nick, Homage (Buddies in Bad Times Theatre/Shaw Festival); Claude, 15 Seconds (Prairie Theatre Exchange); Luc, The Orphan Muses (Great Canadian Theatre Company); Grave Digger, Hamlet (Arts Club); and Elvis, Picasso at the Lampin Agile (Vancouver Playhouse/Grand Theatre). Selected Film and TV credits: the soon to be released feature movie, The Returned, Flashpoint (CTV), Beauty and the Beast (CBS), Covert Affairs (USA Network), The Border (CTV), The Bridge (CBC), Zack Files (YTV); Second String (TNT); PSI Factor, Ordeal in the Arctic (Alliance Atlantis) and Down Came the Rain (CFRN).

www.rogershank.com

www.ingramcontent.com/pod-product-compliance
Lightning Source LLC
Chambersburg PA
CBHW051710040426
42446CB00008B/810